flag

waves

Four Corners Books

flag

**House Flags from the National Maritime Museum
by Sue Prichard**

waves

Introduction by Sue Prichard   6

The Flags   23

Introduction by Sue Prichard

For centuries, flags have been an important part of a ship's identity and communication. Flags might indicate the ship's national origin, rank, or owner, citations received as well as a complex system of codes that could convey detailed messages. These could veer from the everyday, such as signalling an intention to leave port, to the highly charged, indicating that a ship is in distress. This signalling system relied on an arrangement of geometric shapes used in formation, the most famous example is that used by Nelson at the Battle of Trafalgar in which flags were used to signal to his ships the message 'England expects that every man will do his duty'.

House flags are the markers used to aid identification of the company, organisation or individual who owns a ship — over time, thousands of shipping companies have operated across the globe. Some were short-lived and employed only a handful of vessels, whereas others are long-established with vast fleets.

Somewhat surprisingly, house flags were rarely flown at sea, instead being raised when leaving and entering port, and occasionally during the period of their stay: owners could quickly and easily identify their own ships amongst the heavily congested ports. At sea it was possible to distinguish between the ships of certain lines by the decoration of the funnel, which was often a pared-down form of the house flag design (although by no means did every company employ unique funnel livery). This area of maritime corporate identity might seem an unlikely source of striking designs, but the visual language of flags—mostly consisting of a seemingly never-ending combination of geometric shapes and bold, primary colours—both anticipates and has much in common with some of the avant-garde art movements of the twentieth century.

On the whole, house flag design has not depended on prevailing styles or trends and this is perhaps the reason why flags have been largely neglected within the wider context of art and design history. However, the diversity to be found in this collection demonstrates the enormous creativity of the often unknown individuals working with a tight framework of colours, letters and symbols. With a few exceptions, they were produced in an era before the advent of in-house design studios or with access to commercial advertising or branding agencies. Broadly speaking, house flags fall into a number of overlapping stylistic categories: designs drawn from heraldry; geometric forms; the initials of the company or shipowner; a corporate logo; a rebus form of pictograms relating to the activity of the company or organisation; or an adaptation of a pre-existing flag, such as an ensign. This rather limited visual vocabulary proved endlessly versatile, allowing thousands of individual designs to be produced simply by changing an initial, altering the colour, or choosing a circle instead of a square, or a triangle or a diamond.

Over the centuries there have been many types and styles of flag design, however, the fundamental structure of a flag is based on the medieval conventions of heraldry. Vexillology (the study of flags) and heraldry are, therefore, two branches of the same discipline and ultimately the antecedents of this rich and complex armorial system forms the basis of all the designs illustrated in this publication. The house flag of the Hindustan Steam Shipping Co. Ltd, is a simple but visually arresting arrangement of four quartered fields of colour. While the flag nods to the pageantry of the past, its aesthetic appeal also speaks to the formal arrangement of lines, shapes and colours employed by the Dutch

pioneer of abstraction Piet Mondrian (1872–1944). Primarily produced between the mid-nineteenth and mid-twentieth centuries, these flags have a unique visual appeal; indeed, some of the simplest designs exhibit startling effects of bold, graphic originality.

The history and culture of flags

Vexillology is a relatively modern term used to describe the study of flags. It was first conceived and used in 1957 by the American Whitney Smith (1940–2016). Smith was instrumental in establishing the Flag Research Center (1962) and co-founded the International League of Vexillologists (1965), subsequently replaced by the International Federation of Vexillogical Associations (FIAV) in 1969. The FIAV flag, designed by Klaes Siersma, shows a bold yellow sheet bend knot against a blue ground. In common with other disciplines such as architecture, flag design has its own vocabulary and specialised terms. The basic elements of a flag are the badge, canton, charge, emblem, field, fimbriation, finial, fly, hoist, length, width or breadth. The most correct way to describe the FIAV flag is, therefore, 'on a blue field, extending horizontally from hoist to fly, two yellow halyards forming two interlaced loops'. For further precision, the colour blue is defined as Pantone Matching System U293 and the colour yellow is U123.

Flags have existed throughout the centuries and different cultures have developed their own distinct symbols and motifs. From Egypt to Ancient Rome, flags defined social status and importance within a strictly regulated hierarchy. Flags flown today have changed little in basic form or essential function from those flown in the Middle Ages and earlier. Today, as in the past, the flag remains a uniquely telling symbol of identity and loyalty. Its origins reside on the battlefield and safeguarding it from enemy capture was a matter of great honour and bloody sacrifice. There are numerous accounts across the centuries of supreme acts of courage and sacrifice in defending 'the colours'. One of the smallest fragments in the National Maritime Museum collection is a seemingly insignificant fragment of woven wool. It is one of many fragments of the Union Jack flown by <u>Victory</u>, Nelson's flagship at the Battle of Trafalgar on 21 October 1805.

The flag returned with Nelson's body and was used to drape his coffin in the funeral procession from Greenwich Hospital to Whitehall and then to St Paul's Cathedral held on 8–9 January 1806. At the culmination of the ceremony, as the coffin was about to descend into the crypt, a wave of collective grief and emotion took hold of the ordinary seamen who attended the coffin. A contemporary account reports: 'These brave fellows, however, desirous of retaining some memorials of their great and favourite commander, had torn off a considerable part of the largest flag, of which most of them obtained a portion.' This example says as much about national identity as it does regarding the phenomenon of mass hysteria. These tiny remnants of woven fabric, faded with age and by much handling signal our continuing engagement with an object of emotion, symbolic of our continuing quest to connect to the past.

The African-Guyanese playwright, poet and children's writer John Agard interrogates this theme in his 2006 poem <u>Flag</u>. Agard, born in 1949 in the colony of British Guiana (present day Guyana), grew up under the British Blue Ensign with the colonial badge in the fly. The design was used across the Commonwealth, and is still used by the Board of Trade. A new design by professional vexillogist Whitney Smith, slightly modified by the British College of Arms, was adopted on 26 May 1966 to celebrate Guyana's independence from British rule.

BOARD OF TRADE

In vexillogical terms, 'The Golden Arrowhead' is described as 'a green field with the black-edged red isosceles triangle based on the hoist-side superimposed on the large white-edged golden triangle, also based on the hoist side, pointed toward the fly side'. This is perhaps a somewhat stark description for an object that symbolises the rich landscape of Guyana and the enduring attributes of its people, as well as celebrating the country's independence from a colonial power. While not specifically referencing either the British Blue Ensign or 'The Golden Arrowhead',

Agard's poem nevertheless gets to the emotional nub of our relationship with flags. Defined as 'just a piece of cloth', a flag has innate power, one that 'brings a nation to its knees' and 'dares the coward to relent'.

Art and fashion historian Christopher Breward wrote 'the effects of empire can still be witnessed with the superimposition of an overarching identity on much older regional and national identities'. Independence from colonial powers offers countries new opportunities to create new flags based on their own cultural heritage. However, as a symbol of sovereignty, the British ensign is capable of provoking conflicting, and in some cases, extreme emotions. This was made apparent in the 2016 New Zealand referendum on a proposed new flag for the country. Formally adopted in 1902 but in use since 1869, the flag of New Zealand is based on the British Blue Ensign defaced by four red five-pointed stars, symbolising the Southern Cross constellation. It was originally designed in 1869 by the British explorer, author and naval officer Admiral Sir Albert Hastings Markham (1841–1918).

In 2016, New Zealand's then Prime Minister, John Key, championed a new flag by the architectural designer Kyle Lockwood. Of Māori descent, Lockwood's design features a silver fern on a blue and black background, its pinnate form representing New Zealand's multicultural society, while retaining the original arrangement of stars of the Southern Cross. However, Lockwood's new palette favours colours traditionally associated with the Māori people rather than referencing those of the old ensign. Key acknowledged the importance of Lockwood's new design: 'It is quite hard to get an entire nation represented on a piece of cloth. I do see it as a work of art and it is also something that should represent all of us.' Despite being shortlisted in the first referendum, in the second vote the New Zealand public decided 56.7% in favour of retaining the 1902 flag, as opposed to 43.3% for the new design.

One of the most culturally significant flags of the twenty-first century is that used by the environmental movement Extinction Rebellion (XR). As a symbol that addresses complex geopolitical issues such as global warming, the flag has gained international recognition via the media. Originally designed by the East London street artist, ESP, the bold black 'extinction symbol' of two triangles set within a circle represents the planet and a stylised hourglass. With its use of a limited palette of bright colours and concise but carefully worded slogans, the visual impact of the designs has been recognised by the Victoria and Albert Museum. A digital version of the symbol was acquired as part of the V&A's Rapid Response Collecting programme and they likened it to the success of the Suffragette campaigns of the early twentieth century. The National Maritime Museum also acquired a collection of ten flags used by Extinction Rebellion on the protest boat Polly Higgins. It was used during their summer 2019 protests calling for urgent action against climate change. The boat was subsequently loaned to the Museum and displayed on the front lawn, complete with flags. In addition to the zero-extinction logo in white, neon green and neon pink, the protest group used block printed images of marine creatures including a turtle, shrimp, octopus, cod and seahorse. A skull flag was also used. Primarily used in demonstrations, the Extinction Rebellion flags remind us of our evolving relationship with the sea and the public's increasing concern of our impact on the oceans.

House flag design: harking back to heraldry and mirroring modernity

From ancient times and across many cultures, flags have been used both as a symbol of loyalty and as a communication tool. While there are many types and styles of flags, fundamentally their form and function has changed little over the centuries. Traditionally constructed from woven cloth or silk, few early examples have survived the rigours of time. Some knowledge of the types of standards and gonfalons, or banners, used to assemble and lead troops can be gleaned from illustrated manuscripts. However, the Bayeux Tapestry, one of the most important textiles in the world, is also a significant visual record of the style and design of medieval flags. Made some twenty years after the Battle of Hastings (1066), it depicts King Harold's standard featuring a red wyvern, a two-legged winged dragon with barbed tail frequently used in heraldry. In contrast,

William the Conqueror's flag is depicted as a variation on the gonfalon, with three tails in green and yellow featuring a gold cross in the centre, with four yellow balls in its corners. The cross is used extensively in heraldry and is known as the Jerusalem cross, 'five-fold Cross' or 'cross-and-crosslets', in which the large cross is typically surrounded by four smaller Greek crosses. In simplified form, the cross was adopted and used during the twelfth-century Crusades. Within Western Europe the red cross of St George has featured prominently on a number of flags.

Unlike the vast array of colours available via the Pantone Matching System used today, heraldic colours, or 'tinctures', are extremely limited. They consist of only single shades within two basic categories: colours and metals. 'Colours' are defined as red (gules), black (sable), blue (azure), green (vert) and purple (purpure). 'Metals' are defined as gold (or) and silver (argent), although these definitions are expanded to include orange and yellow, and white and grey respectively. Strict rules dictated the use of these colours whereby metal cannot be placed over metal, or colour on colour.

Many house flag designs draw on this rich history of heraldry to reflect their company's core values. The complex arrangement of geometric motifs, plants, animals and mythological beasts within a framework of lines and colours speak eloquently to notions of tradition and heritage, alongside individual nationality and identity. The flag of the Central Electricity Generating Board features a rather fine red griffin with yellow talons and beak, which has been adapted from the crest of the board's coat of arms. Used widely in corporate logos, a mythological beast can symbolise leadership and strength, as well as military prowess. In the same vein, many flags employ a heraldic lion as their badge. Within the heraldic structure, lines are used to create divisions. These lines can have many different shapes, including serrated and wavy. Traditionally used to denote

CENTRAL ELECTRICITY GENERATING BOARD

water, the wavy line is a popular motif in flag design. The striking but simple house flag of the Orkney Steam Navigation Co. employs lines to great effect. The rectangular flag is divided diagonally into four broad white stripes and five narrow red stripes. These bold horizontal or vertical lines anticipate the Op Art movement of the 1960s, and the seminal paintings of Bridget Riley. Within the conventions of vexillology, lines in flag design follow a rigid system of scientific exactitude. If the lines are of equal width, only the number of lines will be described. However, if the design consists of lines of unequal size, a numerical sequence would be used. So for example, if the middle stripe is twice as wide as each of the outer stripes this would be described as 1:1:2:1:1.

ORKNEY STEAM NAVIGATION COMPANY

Designed principally to communicate visually across distance, many flags share the bold characteristics associated with modernist sensibilities. While geometric symbols have been used throughout antiquity, a preoccupation with abstraction dominated much of the art and design of the early twentieth century. In Europe and Revolutionary Russia artists sought to dispense with historical and cultural associations of the past in a quest for a more democratic approach to design. The flag of Cory Colliers Ltd, for example, consists of a red rectangle with a white diamond in the centre. This stark simplicity adheres to the Austrian and Czech architect and theorist Adolf Loos's polemic that decoration was 'superfluous to the needs of the rational modern age'. Throughout the 1920s, lack of decorative detail and the quest for a universal or visual language became the hallmark of the Bauhaus Staatlichen Schule für Gestaltung, where Paul Klee, László Moholy-Nagy and Wassily Kandinsky all taught. The house

CORY COLLIERS LTD

flag of Lambert Brothers Ltd, a white rectangular flag with red triangle in the centre, and of the Currie Line, London, a white saltire (diagonal cross-shape) above a white cross, reflect the German art and design school's preference for reduced, simplified forms. In his Bauhaus textbook, Kandinsky advocated a 'dictionary of elements' based on a vocabulary of elementary forms of circles, squares and triangles. As a universal means of communication, the geometric shapes on many house flags recall the innovative textile designs emerging from the Bauhaus and from avant-garde artists in Revolutionary Russia. The simple white disc on the red pennant of the Belfast Steam Ship Co. Ltd prefigures the approach of the Bauhaus weaving workshop, pioneered by Gunta Stölzl (1897–1983) and Anni Albers (1899–1994), which eschewed traditional pictorial designs in favour of abstract and geometric patterns.

Sometimes heraldry and geometry come together. The house flag of Strick Line Ltd, London, for example, employs the chevron, one of the earliest geometric symbols used in heraldry. This flag, and the single white star on the swallow-tailed pennant of the White Star Line recall the radical egalitarian sportswear designs of the mid-1920s by the Constructivist artist, philosopher and graphic designer Varvara Stepanova (1894–1954).

While it is possible, therefore, in a retrospective sense, to see modernism within the design of house flags, it is unlikely that this represents anything more than a coincidence stemming from the desire to have a flag that was cheap and simple to produce, and recognisable.

In terms of design and decoration, passenger liners may have been in step with the latest trends, but flags for tramp steamers, oil tankers and tugs were not afforded such attention. The story of the 'design' in 1824 of a house flag for the London firm of Wigram and Green is telling. Originally intended to be a square St George's flag, the commanding admiral at Portsmouth objected as it offended naval tradition. To appease the Royal Navy's sensibilities, a simple solution was found by stitching a blue handkerchief over the middle. Two versions of this basic and swiftly improvised design were employed by different Wigram and Green companies throughout the nineteenth century: a blue square under the cross was the flag of Green's 'Blackwall Line' and the ships of Money Wigram and Sons had a flag with the blue square over the cross.

THE STRICK LINE

Employing a design consultancy to create a brand or logo is a relatively recent phenomenon. 'House style', now more commonly known as 'corporate identity', was essentially an unknown concept in the late nineteenth and early twentieth centuries and pioneered by a small number of organisations like London Underground, which adhered to a clear set of design principles. Designers Milner Gray, Misha Black and Marcus Brumwell, along with the art historian Herbert Read, established the influential Design Research Unit (1943). Grey oversaw the makeover of the newly nationalised British Railways in 1948, employing a stylised lion and engine wheel to evoke a strong sense of power and history as the old identities of the earlier companies like LNER and Great Western disappeared. In 1965, the faltering company was rebranded as British Rail and a new logo was adopted of white interlocked arrows on a red ground. This design was

THE WHITE STAR LINE

placed on a blue ground for use on Sealink ferries, which were an extension of the British Rail network. This exercise was part of a 1960s trend whereby design agencies were producing manuals specifying when and where logotypes and brand colours would be used. Shipping was not immune to the efforts to systematise corporate identity and many long-established shipping names, which retained their old identities as part of larger companies, began to disappear in the second half of the twentieth century as the industry consolidated and changed.

All the examples in the collection illustrate the challenge in creating a clear, crisp design that can be read at a distance. Some are clearly more successful than others, however, the best designs achieve a balance between clarity of purpose, symbol and text. In some cases, the simple expedient of a single letter or alphabetical arrangement of letters conveys the message. In contrast to house flags, the Museum's collection of pleasure yacht ensigns and burgees rely on simple monograms such as RYS (Royal Yacht Squadron) or the name of the individual owner and their club. This typographical approach is limited to a simple san serif format with little tonal texture.

House flags: production, promotion and permutation

Unlike other areas of textile production, flags have not been subject to major technological developments in manufacture. Created before the introduction of computer software, flags were hand made from woven cloth, and the designs were then either printed or appliquéd. By the late nineteenth century, the majority of house flags were produced using industrial methods and competition was intense. Numerous companies produced house flags, burgees and Union Jacks in addition to church and business flags and bunting 'ready for Festooning'. Some manufacturers specialised in supplying 'stock' patterns which could then be augmented with a particular company's initials or logo. Tutill's, based at 83 City Road, London, functioned as a government contractor and produced house flags 'Made of Double Warp All Wool Bunting, of Good Quality, and Pattern Dyed in Permanent Fast Colours'. Wilkinson & Co. had its office in Liverpool and boasted they were contractors for the Admiralty and War Office. Piggott Bros. & Co. of Bishopsgate, London were established in 1780. In addition to supplying 'Flags of all Nations', they also provided flagstaffs to various organisations, including the British Museum, the India Office and Selfridges on Oxford Street, which had nineteen.

Historically, the Admiralty provided regular updates on new designs and changes to existing flags. In the eighteenth and early nineteenth centuries flag charts were issued on paper sheets or instructional booklets displaying maritime flags. Surviving examples tend to be rare, however, books describing shipping company flags and funnels can still be found in libraries and archives and provide a wealth of information on some of the more obscure shipping lines. Lloyd's List of House Flags was first published 1882. A 'notice' in the book carried the following caveat:

> The Compilers are fully aware that this First Edition may contain errors and omissions, and in gratefully acknowledging the courteous assistance they have received from the Ship Owners of the United Kingdom, confidently hope that a continuance of such help will enable them to make the Second Edition more perfect.

Together with the subsequent Lloyd's Book of House Flags and Funnels (1904 and 1912), these reference works are evocative reminders of the heyday of mercantile trade and are collectible objects in their own right. They pay testament to the extraordinary number of designs produced from a simple design vocabulary over a relatively short period. The 1912 edition of Lloyd's contains 448 more flags and funnels than the previous edition published some eight years earlier. The sheer number of permutations of designs based on, for example, a saltire or a white circle on a red or blue ground demonstrate the utility of these comprehensive identification guides. In addition to Lloyd's, a small number of independent publishers also issued illustrated books designed to help identify flags flown by the Royal Navy as well as the merchant marine. Moreover, they contained instructions for identifying international codes and information on the sound signals for fog and the all-important signals of distress. Examples of such publications, which frequently ran to many subsequent editions, include: <u>Flags National and Mercantile; for the use of Officers of Royal Navy, Merchant Marine; and Yacht Squadrons</u>, compiled by James Griffin (Portsmouth: Griffin & Co., 1883): <u>Reed's House Flags and Funnels of English and Foreign Steamship Companies</u> (Sunderland: Thomas Reed & Co., 1890); <u>Brown's Flags and Funnels of British and Foreign Steamship Companies</u>, compiled by Captain F.J.N. Wedge (Glasgow: Brown, Son & Ferguson, 1926); <u>House Flags and Funnels of British and Foreign Shipping Companies</u>, drawn and edited by E. C. Talbot-Booth (London: Sampson Low, Marston, 1937); Colin Stewart, <u>Flags, Funnels and Hull Colours</u> (London: Adlard Coles, 1953); and <u>A Survey of Mercantile Houseflags and Funnels</u>, edited by J. L. Loughran (Wolverhampton: Waine Research, 1979). In addition, <u>The Liverpool Journal of Commerce</u> published a number of charts depicting house flags and funnels.

In an interesting departure from the norm, charts were also produced as silk squares printed in full colour. These colourful textiles are again extremely collectable as well as being helpful in dating flags. The Museum has two examples, the earliest dates from 1817–29 and features the Hanoverian Royal Coat of Arms (1817–37) in an attractive design. The British Royal Standard consists of four quarters, one with a harp, one with a lion rampant and two with three lions passant, thus combining the ancient royal emblems of Ireland, Scotland and England respectively. After 1837 and the accession of Queen Victoria, the Hanoverian Standard was replaced by the Victorian version. Changes in government as well as monarch offered up opportunities for adapting flags and introducing new designs. In an unidentified newspaper clipping pasted into the Caird Library copy of <u>Lloyd's Book of House Flags and Funnels</u> (1912) at the National Maritime Museum, a number of new mercantile flags were described. 'In the Far East we find the Chinese Republic with a new flag, five lengthwise strips, Red, Yellow, Blue, White, Black, a brilliant flag! Egypt also has a brilliant flag, Red ground, with three white half-moons on the left, and each half-moon has a white star'. Here the term 'brilliant' means very bright or dazzling as opposed to marvellous or excellent.

The flag collection at the National Maritime Museum

The National Maritime Museum is home to one of the most internationally significant and diverse collections of flags. Containing more than 1,000 objects, the collection is a colourful and, some might say, emotive reminder of Britain's seafaring past. The variety is bewildering and includes national flags from around the world, not least the Union Jack, naval and merchant ensigns, heraldic banners, royal standards, yacht flags, sledge flags from

COMMONWEALTH STANDARAD

polar expeditions and even flags from naval staff cars as well as the house flags of shipping companies, government departments and other organisations. The earliest, and rarest, complete flag in the collection is a mid-seventeenth-century Commonwealth Standard used by the Generals at Sea, the most senior officers of the Cromwellian navy. Made of red wool bunting with a linen hoist, the flag is hand-sewn with an appliquéd design showing a wreath of laurel and bay branches surrounding two shields charged with the cross of St George and the harp of Ireland. During this turbulent political period, the Royal Standard and Union Flag that symbolised the unification of the crowns of England and Scotland were replaced by a variety of devices based on the cross of St George impaling the Irish harp. Hastily constructed to reflect the change in loyalties from crown to state, the flag is thus a tangible reminder of the sometimes transient nature of political regimes. The flag also represents the dangers of a speedy adoption of new and unfamiliar iconography: it has been made with the shields upside down.

As one might expect, the collection primarily focuses on the flags of the Royal Navy and the merchant fleet. With regard to the latter, two major acquisitions form the bulk of the house flag collection. The first was acquired in 1967 from Mrs A. Gladys Pope, widow of Charles Meredyth Pope. Between 1917 and 1967, he assembled an extraordinary collection of 273 British house flags, representing the diversity of design across this period. The second collection, largely assembled by Daniel Roberts Bolt, a borough official in Poplar, comprises nearly 140 flags of shipping lines collected in the first decade of the twentieth century. Most are made of traditional wool bunting and were originally on loan from the London Borough of Tower Hamlets for many years before finally being acquired in 2009. Mindful of the lack of public memorials of Britain's mercantile fleet, in 1911 Poplar Library officials assembled a collection of house flags of well-known shipping houses as 'a permanent record of the doings of famous ships and famous men'. The collecting policy focused on house flags of 'those firms whose ships have traded to Poplar' and the collection

COMMISSIONERS OF IRISH LIGHTS

was exhibited at Poplar Recreation Ground in June 1911 in celebration of the coronation of King George V. These two collections illustrate the vast range of designs employed to represent shipping lines and maritime organisations. In the Pope Collection, for example, is the flag of the Commissioners of the Irish Lights, the authority responsible for lighthouses in Ireland. Unlike the vast majority of house flags, which rely on geometric motifs, this design consists of a red St George's cross on a white ground with a painting of lighthouse and lightship in alternative cantons. By contrast, in the Bolt collection is the simple, but rather unusual house flag of J.P. Corry & Co., London (Star Line Limited, circa 1911), which features a red heart at the centre. Leonard Potts, the Town Clerk responsible for writing the 1911 exhibition catalogue, provides an evocative reminder of the spectacle of large fleets

J.P. CORRY & CO.

of merchant ships on the Thames: 'Amongst the large fleets of sailing ships that are now no more, the "Irish Stars", as they were familiarly called, were of high magnitude. They were splendid ships, and were well-known in the South West India Dock.' It is intriguing why the Corry family of Ulster, which founded the Star Line eschewed the rather obvious choice of a star in favour of a traditionally more romantic symbol.

Flags are a fundamental part of our maritime heritage. While several publications have been written on the history of flags at sea, this is the first to focus on their pattern and design. The National Maritime Museum collection is a rich source of material in which new and sometimes surprising discoveries can be made. Colourful and eclectic, the house flag is an example of the extraordinary creativity preserved within a maritime context. The designs adhere to the ethos espoused by the designer Raymond Loewry (1893–1986): 'more than function itself, simplicity is the deciding factor in the aesthetic equation… beauty through function and simplification'.

American Mail Line
House flag, Seattle, USA, c. 1955
made by Puget Sound Tent and Duck Co., printed, machine sewn
91.4 × 152 cm

FLAG WAVES

Anchor Line Ltd (formed in 1899, formerly Handysides & Henderson)
House flag, Glasgow, c. 1955
unknown maker, machine sewn
121.9 × 182.9 cm

FLAG WAVES

Australind Steam Shipping Co. Ltd (formed 1904)
House flag, London, c. 1951
unknown maker, machine sewn
121.9 × 182.9 cm

Baltic Trading Co. Ltd
House flag, London, *c.* 1951
unknown maker, machine sewn
121.9 × 187.9 cm

Bamburgh Shipping Co. Ltd (formed 1956)
House flag, Newcastle-upon-Tyne, *c.* 1956–1967
unknown maker, machine sewn
91.4 × 142.2 cm

Belfast Steam Ship Co. Ltd (formed 1852)
House flag, Belfast, c. 1955
unknown maker, machine sewn
121.9 × 198.1 cm

FLAG WAVES

Coast Development Corporation Ltd (Belle Steamers)
House flag, London (Buff Funnel Line), dates from before 1937
unknown maker, machine sewn
180.3 × 276.8 cm

FLAG WAVES

Bibby Brothers and Co.
House flag, Liverpool, c. 1955–1967
unknown maker, machine sewn
147.3 × 215.9 cm

32

The colour red was traditionally associated with empire and royalty. However, from the 19th century onwards the plain red flag has been increasingly identified as a symbol of protest. It was first used during the French Revolution and was adopted as the official flag of the 1871 Paris Commune. In 1918, the red banner with the initials of the state in the upper left corner was adopted by the newly formed Russian Socialist Federated Soviet Republic, later the Soviet Union.

In 1872 the Bibby family sold their shipping interest to Frederick Leyland & Co. Ltd. The Leyland Line house flag was a plain red rectangle. In 1889 the Bibby family returned to the shipping business, initially as Bibby Brothers Ltd and later changing its name to the Bibby Steamship Company. It operated 'fast twin-screw mail steamers to Marseilles, Egypt, Colombo, South India and Burma, and passenger cruises and tours to the Mediterranean'. In 1912 Lloyd's Book of House Flags and Funnels lists the Bibby Bros & Co. (Bibby Line) house flag as a plain red rectangle. In 1926 a Bibby Line ship was detained in Hamburg. Confusion had arisen as the house flag was mistaken with that of the Soviet Union. As a result, the Bibby family crest of an erect yellow hand holding a similar coloured dagger was added to the original plain flag to avoid association with Bolshevism.

FLAG WAVES

Boston Deep Sea Fishing and Ice Co. Ltd (formed 1885)
House flag, Boston, Lincolnshire, c. 1955
unknown maker, machine sewn
86.3 × 137.1 cm

34

FLAG WAVES

Bowater Steamship Co. (formed 1955)
House flag, London, unknown date
unknown maker, machine sewn
142.2 × 279.4 cm

The pale blue rectangular flag with an applied motif of two parallel rails and arrows pointing in opposite directions was the brainchild of designer Gerry Barney. Prior to 1948, individual railway companies had their own crests. Following rail nationalisation in 1948, the British Railways crest, or 'totem', featured a yellow lion astride a red wheel, facing forward on both sides of the locomotive. In 1960, the Design Research Unit received the brief to design a new logo for the reconstituted British Rail, which came into being in 1963. Barney, who worked with Milner Gray, initially sketched his idea 'on the back of an envelope'. The DRU shortlisted Barney's design from 50 different symbols. Alongside the symbol, the DRU also created a logotype and a palette of house colours.

The shipping services of Britain's railway companies were born out of a desire to continue services beyond the coastline. Routes were operated to the Continent, Ireland, the Channel Islands, the Western Isles of Scotland and the Isle of Wight. British Rail Shipping and International Services was formed in 1968. Links to continental rail and shipping companies brought about the formation of Sealink in 1970.

For those familiar with the British Rail logo, it appears to be the 'wrong' way round: it is used in a reversed form on one side of the flag so that the top arrow would always point towards the flag staff. The top arrow of the logo on the funnel would always point towards the bows of the ship.

British Rail
House flag, 1967
Designed by Gerry Barney, machine sewn
121.9 × 182.9 cm

FLAG WAVES

British Waterways Board
House flag, c. 1963–1970
unknown maker, machine sewn
129.5 × 182.9 cm

British Waterways was founded in 1963 and was the navigation authority for most of the inland waterways in the UK until 2012 when it began operating as the Canal & River Trust in England and Wales, and Scottish Canals in Scotland. British Waterways used this paddle wheel motif until 1970 when the design was changed to a wave motif.

Burns and Laird Lines
House flag, Glasgow, c. 1955
unknown maker, machine sewn
149.8 × 203.2 cm

Originally, the house flag of G. & J. Burns Ltd (which began operating under that name in 1842), the company was amalgamated with Laird Lines in 1922.

Cable and Wireless (Marine) Ltd
House flag, London, 1987
unknown maker, machine sewn
121.9 × 185.4 cm

This flag is emblematic of the Golden Fleece Line's trade. Made from wool, the design employs a white saltire to divide the red field into four parts. The charming central emblem of the golden fleece has been hand painted in yellow.

All the ships of the Golden Fleece Line were named after characters in The Argonautica, a 3rd century BC Greek poem by Apollonius Rhodius. It recounts the legendary journey of Jason and his crew of doughty Argonauts in their quest for the Golden Fleece. They were assisted by Medea, daughter of King Aeetes of Colchis.

This flag was flown on the three-masted, iron clipper Mermerus, which was launched in 1872 and named after the son of Jason and Medea. On its return maiden voyage from Melbourne to England, Mermerus carried 10,000 bales of wool, equivalent to the fleeces of over a million sheep. The ship remained in service until 1910. The Golden Fleece was a popular symbol associated with the wool trade. In the 18th and 19th centuries, intricately carved and gilded wooden signs hung outside woollen drapers shops, providing a highly visible means of identifying a tradesman's business.

A. and J.H. Carmichael, Greenock (Golden Fleece Line)
House flag, c. 1872–1910
unknown maker, painted, machine sewn
182.8 × 228.6 cm

The Central Electricity Generating Board (CEGB) flag uses the heraldic motif of a griffin, a hybrid beast combining the attributes of two of the most majestic creatures of land and air with the body, tail and back legs of a lion and the head and wings of an eagle. This combination meant the griffin was considered to be especially powerful in mythology. This striking flag is divided into three fields of red, black and yellow and uses the same colours to delineate the central motif.

The lion's body, head and legs are depicted in red, one of the earliest colours, or tinctures, to be used in heraldry. Yellow, one of the two metals of the heraldic palette, is used for the beak, talons and claws of the eagle, while the black outlines create more definition to the body of the griffin. The motif is a male griffin, depicted without wings but with a small red horn and yellow spikes, the latter giving the impression that the beast is sparking with electricity.

The CEGB was formed in 1958 and was responsible for the supply of electricity to most of England and Wales. Its fleet of ships delivered coal to UK power stations, which in turn supplied the National Grid. The fleet was managed by Stephenson Clarke Ltd, established in 1730 and as such one of Britain's oldest shipping companies. The Stephenson house flag was a red saltire on a blue field with the initials of the company in the four quarters.

Central Electricity Generating Board
House flag, c. 1958–1967
unknown maker, printed, machine sewn
127 × 228.6 cm

FLAG WAVES

Civil Service Sailing Association
Burgee, 1989
unknown maker
33.4 × 53.2 cm

Founded in 1959, the Civil Service Sailing Association's flag design represents a blue anchor fouled with red tape.

Clyde Shipping Co. (formed 1815)
House flag, Glasgow, c. 1951
unknown maker, printed, machine sewn
106.7 × 297.2 cm

This flag design was introduced in 1924 following a suggestion made by Miss Blakiston-Houston. The previous house flag consisted of two red-bordered pennants with the Scottish lion above the Irish harp.

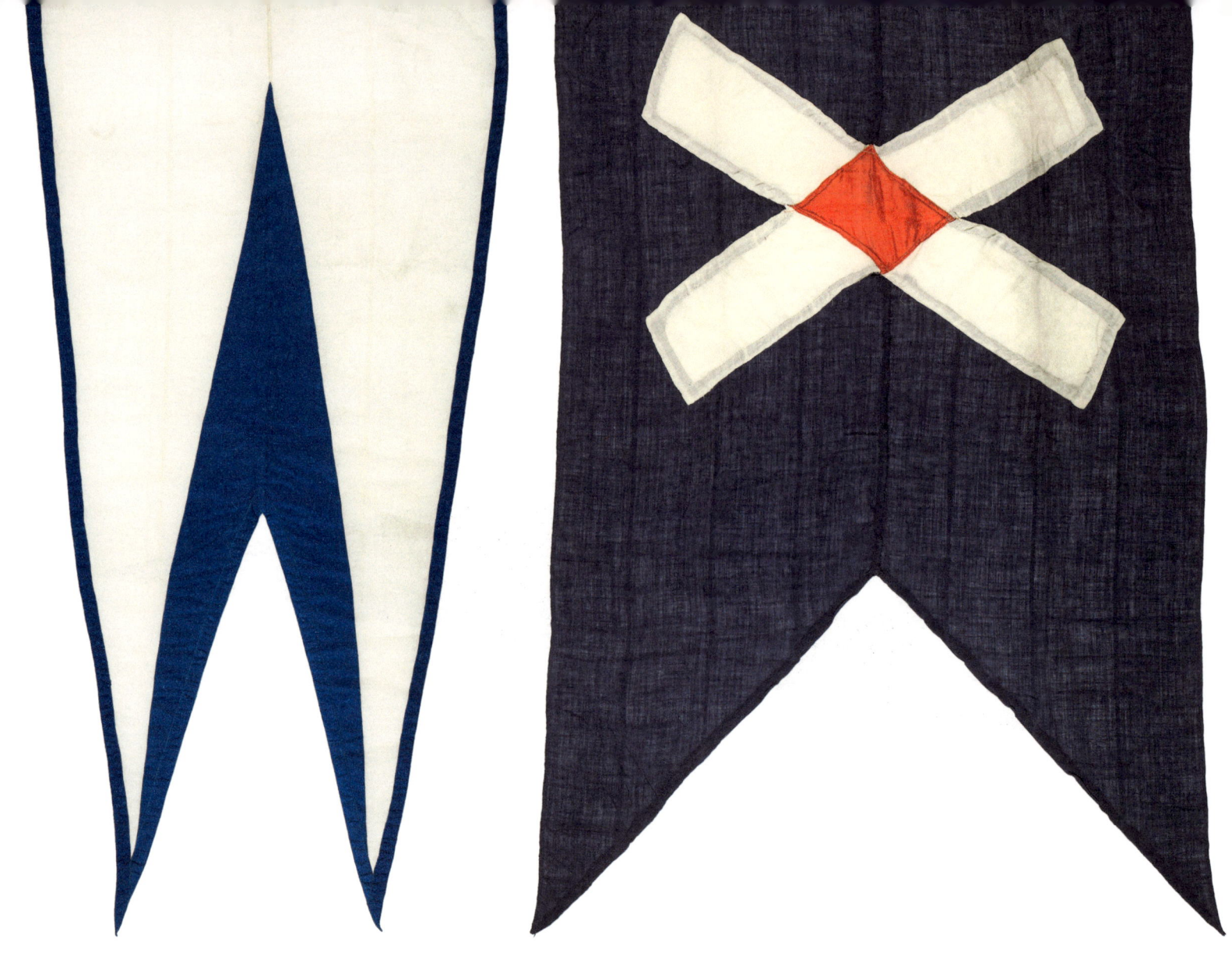

Atlantic Steam Navigation Co. (formed 1934)
House flag, London, *c.* 1955
unknown maker, machine sewn
66 × 152.4 cm

Scottish Shire Line Ltd (formed *c.* 1910)
House flag, *c.* 1951
unknown maker, machine sewn
114.3 × 172.7 cm

David MacBrayne Ltd (formed 1851)
House flag, Glasgow, c. 1955–1967
unknown maker, machine sewn
83.8 × 226 cm

White Star Line (formed 1845)
House flag, Liverpool, c. 1945–1954
unknown maker, machine sewn
101.6 × 182.8 cm

Conservators of the River Thames
Flag, unknown date
made by E. W. Perrett Ltd, machine sewn
127 × 177.8 cm

FLAG WAVES

Constants Ltd
House flag, London, c. 1951
unknown maker, machine sewn
172.7 × 233.7 cm

This rectangular flag bearing a white disc in the centre with a black sans serif letter 'C' is a simple but striking design which has been used by numerous mercantile companies. The flags were manufactured across the country as stock items that could be customised with the owner's or company's initials. Somewhat unusually the hoist has been inscribed 'Constants Cardiff'. The flag formed part of the Pope Collection and the inscription may have been a later addition to help identity the flag.

Constants was a London based company involved in the coal trade since the 18th century. In 1929 it set up a South Wales subsidiary, Constants (South Wales) Ltd. The company ships were all named after Kent villages. Constants exported Welsh coal to southern Europe and the Mediterranean and imported iron ore for the South Wales steel industry. The ships also returned with cork, pyrites and timber from Portugal. From an original fleet of ten, by the end of the Second World War only three ships remained. In the 1950s, the company traded internationally and the fleet was increased to meet demand. Business declined, however, and the company closed in 1976.

Cory Brothers (originally Richard Cory & Sons, formed 1842)
House flag, Cardiff, *c.* 1955–1967
unknown maker, machine sewn
91.4 × 182.8 cm

The red rectangular flag with a white diamond in the centre was flown by William Cory and Son from 1896 to 1985, when the company merged with Cory Towage Limited. The flag was then changed from a white diamond to a blue diamond bordered in white.

    Registered in 1896, William Cory and Son transported over 5 million tonnes of coal every year to the people of London. It operated a fleet of 2,500 railway wagons as well as barges on the Thames. In the First World War, Cory's tugs were requisitioned by the Royal Navy. The company again supported the war effort between 1939 and 1945, transporting much needed fuel supplies. In the 1950s, Cory developed a large fleet of barges specially designed to deal with the vast quantity of waste generated by the population of London. The marshlands of Essex and Kent had been traditional dumping grounds for refuse since the 19th century and by 1970 Cory was the largest transporter of waste on the Thames.

Cory Colliers Ltd
House flag, London, c. 1951
unknown maker, machine sewn
144.7 × 205.7 cm

FLAG WAVES

J. P. Corry & Co. (Star Line Ltd)
House flag, London, c. 1911
unknown maker, machine sewn
190.5 × 264.1 cm

58

Cunard Steamship Co. Ltd (formed 1840)
House flag, Liverpool, *c.* 1951
unknown maker, printed, machine sewn
55.9 × 91.4 cm

FLAG WAVES

Currie Line (formed 1866 as Donald Currie & Co.)
House flag, Leith, c. 1955–1967
unknown maker, machine sewn
134.6 × 264.1 cm

Ellerman's Hall Line Ltd
House flag, Liverpool, c. 1951
unknown maker, printed, machine sewn
Pennant: 68.6 × 177.8 cm, Flag: 114.3 × 177.8 cm

Founded in 1864, originally under the name Robert & Young, the Hall Line was acquired by Ellerman Group in 1901.

FLAG WAVES

Esso Petroleum Co. Ltd
House flag, London and New York, c. 1955–1967
unknown maker, printed, machine sewn
172.7 × 266.7 cm

Founded in 1912, after the breakup of Standard Oil, this version of the Esso logo was in use from 1934 until a revised version was designed in the mid 1960s.

Euxine Shipping Co. (formed 1932)
House flag, London, c. 1951
unknown maker, machine sewn
86.3 × 137.1 cm

FLAG WAVES

W. France, Fenwick & Co.
House flag, London, c. 1955
unknown maker, machine sewn
172.7 × 238.7 cm

This house flag was formerly used by Fenwick, Stobart & Co. before the firm merged with William France in 1901.

Furness Withy & Co.
House flag, London, c. 1951
unknown maker, machine sewn
114.3 × 187.9 cm

Furness Withy was incorporated as a company in 1891 upon the amalgamation of Christopher Furness' business in West Hartlepool and London with Edward Withy's shipbuilding yard in Hartlepool.

FLAG WAVES

Fyffes Group Ltd
House flag, London, c. 1955–1967
unknown maker, machine sewn
180.3 × 276.8 cm

Geest Line Ltd
House flag, Boston, Lincolnshire, 1960s
unknown maker, machine sewn
99 × 147.3 cm

The Van Geest family began as market gardeners in the Netherlands exporting produce to Great Britain. Geest set up a British company in 1935 and acquired land in Lincolnshire. They began chartering ships to carry their fruit and vegetables after the Second World War and formed their own shipping company in 1964.

FLAG WAVES

General Steam Navigation Co. Ltd
House flag, London, c. 1911
unknown maker, printed, machine sewn
142.2 × 223.5 cm

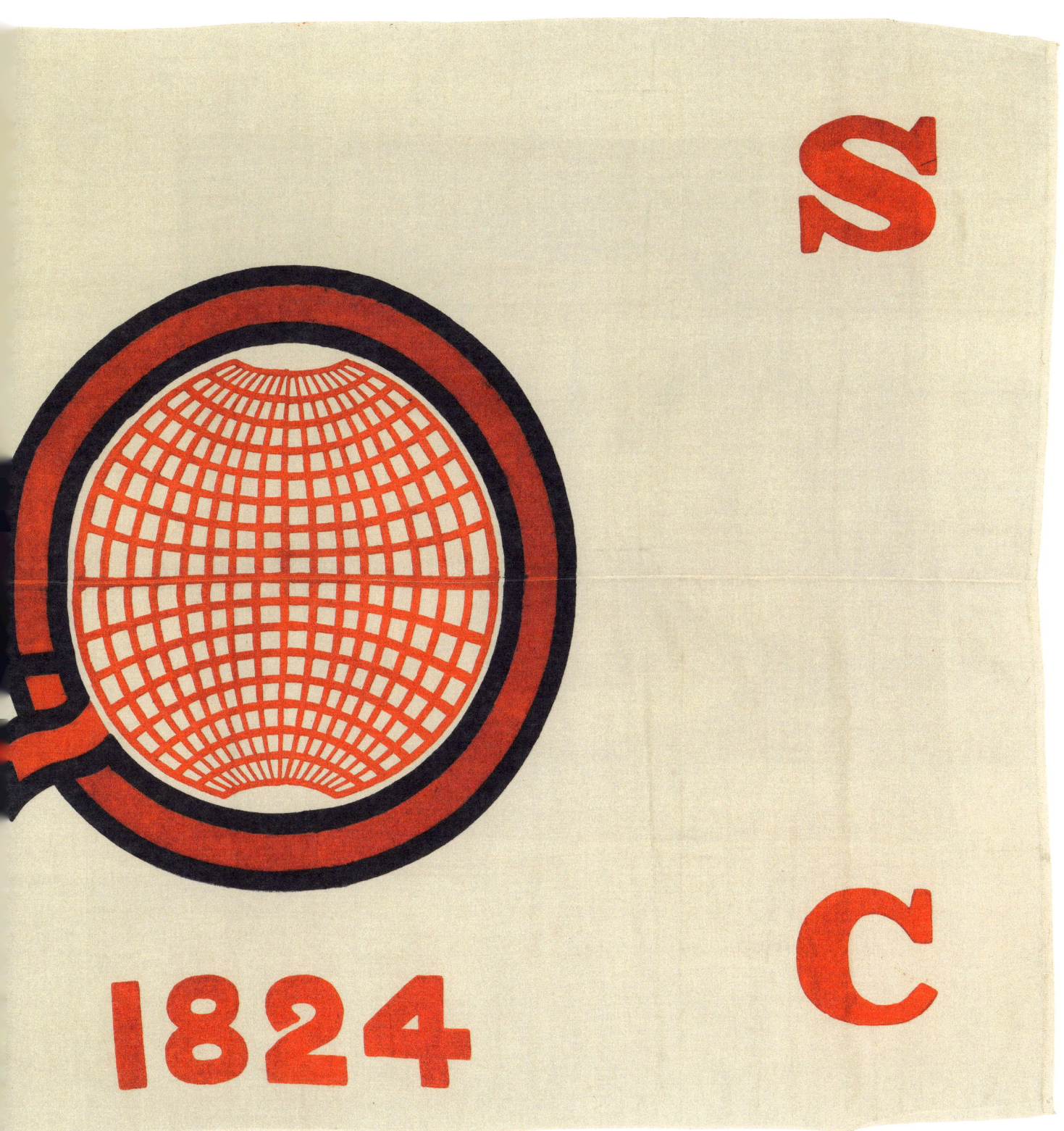

Girl Guides
Flag, unknown date
made by J. Edgington & Co. Ltd, machine sewn
83.8 × 96.5 cm

Grace Brothers and Co. Ltd
House flag, London, c. 1955–1967
unknown maker, machine sewn
116.8 × 185.4 cm

The Greater London Council (GLC) flag is based on the original coat of arms of the London County Council (LCC). The LCC was granted a coat of arms in 1914 and a heraldic badge in 1956. The design was 'simple in character and in every way suggestive of the corporate life of London'. It employed the traditional device of five wavy lines representing the River Thames and Port of London. The red cross of St George against a white field with a yellow lion in the centre represents London as the royal centre of England. The shield was topped with a gold mural crown indicating that the arms were those of a municipal body. The shield of arms of the GLC, granted in 1966, retains the wavy lines of the LCC arms but replaces the cross and lion with the Saxon crown of Middlesex: a device which embraces the GLC's wider geographical responsibility. This flag was used on the Woolwich Ferry, a passenger and vehicle service across the River Thames. The GLC was abolished in 1985.

Greater London Council
House flag, unknown date
unknown maker, printed, machine sewn
119.4 × 182.8 cm

FLAG WAVES

Greenpeace
House flag, c. 1984
made by Shipmate, Netherlands, machine sewn
99 × 152.4 cm

74

Govan Shipbuilders Ltd
House flag, Glasgow, c. 1955–1967
made by James Stevenson (Flags) Ltd, machine sewn
116.8 × 185.4 cm

Guinea Gulf Line Ltd (formed 1954)
House flag, Liverpool, c. 1955–1967
unknown maker, machine sewn
43.2 × 60.9 cm

FLAG WAVES

Guinness Co.
House flag, Dublin, c. 1955–1967
unknown maker, machine sewn
91.4 × 182.8 cm

The company purchased its first ship in 1913, the W.M. Barkley and, in 1931, commissioned its first ship, SS Guinness, which was built to carry beer. In 1977 the MV Miranda Guinness was commissioned, the world's first custom-built bulk liquid carrier: in effect a beer tanker. As the company opened breweries worldwide, the fleet went into decline and in 1993 Guinness ceased its tanker operation.

77

FLAG WAVES

Hadley Shipping Co. Ltd (formed 1926)
House flag, London, c. 1951
unknown maker, machine sewn
192.1 × 182.9 cm

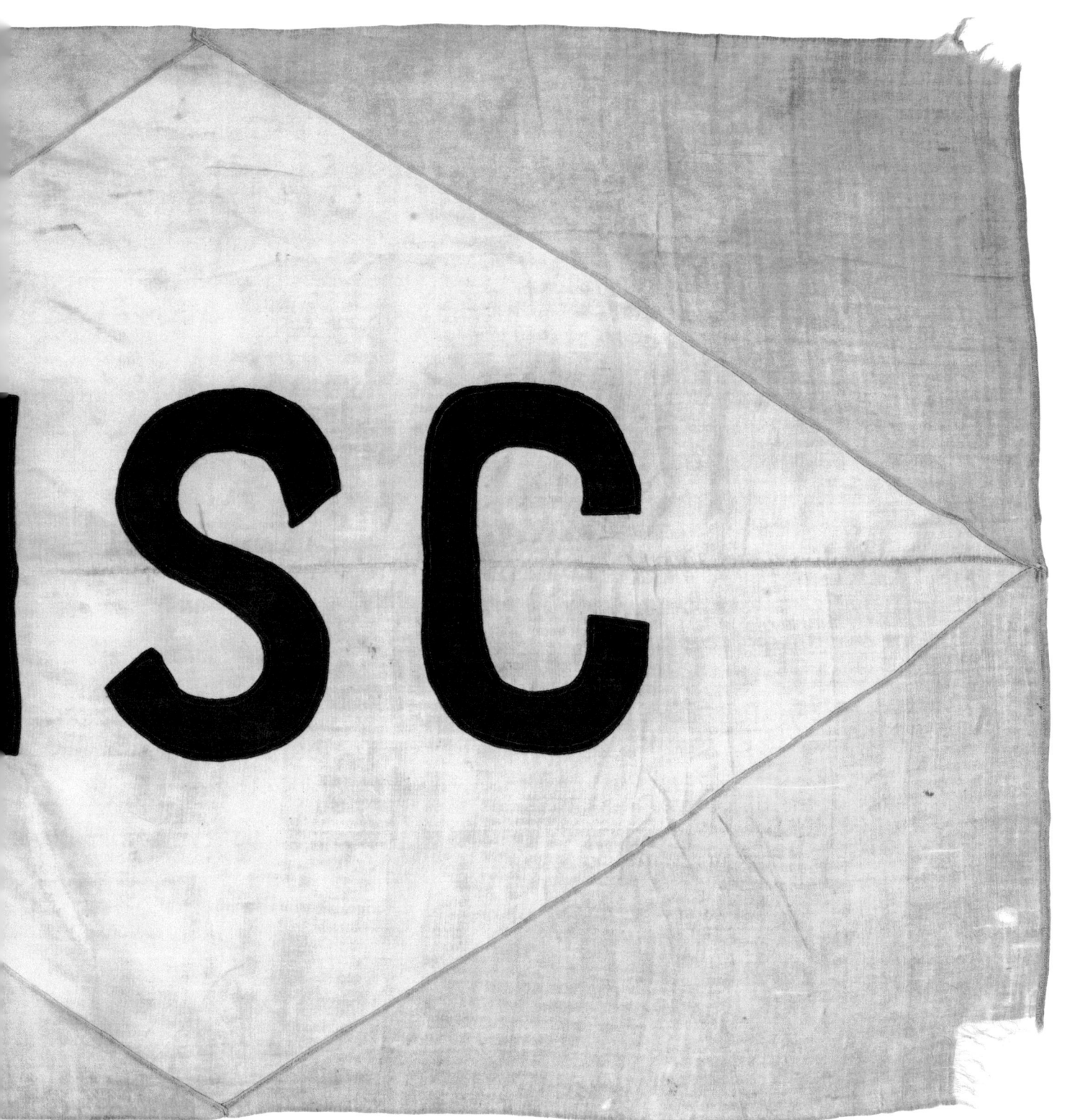

In 1912, the house flag of Hain Steamship Co. Ltd (E. Hain & Son) was a rectangular red flag bearing the initials 'E H' (Edward Hain) in white letters. The James Nourse Ltd, London house flag was a rectangular white flag with blue saltire with red diamond in the centre. The Hain Nourse house is a modern interpretation of the origins and combines elements of both flags: the red, white and blue of Nourse with the conjoined sans serif letters 'HN' in red.

The Hain Steamship Company originated in the small fishing port of St Ives, Cornwall and expanded rapidly to become one of the major shipping companies of the 19th century. It exported cured fish to the Mediterranean, returning with dried fruit. By the 1860s Hain ships were trading worldwide and importing sugar from the West Indies and coffee from Brazil. After the death of its founder, Sir Edward Hain, the company was purchased by P&O Steam Navigation Company, but continued to operate under the management of Hain directors. Hain suffered particularly heavy losses during the Second World War, losing a total of 28 ships. In the early 1960s, as part of a rationalisation exercise, P&O merged three of its tramp shipping companies: Hain Steamship Company, James Nourse Ltd and Asiatic Steam Navigation Company Ltd became Hain Nourse Ltd. In 1971 the Hain-Nourse livery and flag ceased to be used and the ships were re-registered under the P&O name in 1972.

Hain Nourse Management Ltd
House flag, London, c. 1955–1967
unknown maker, machine sewn
116.8 × 192.9 cm

FLAG WAVES

Harrisons (Clyde) Ltd
House flag, Glasgow, c. 1956–1967
unknown maker, printed, machine sewn
116.8 × 190.5 cm

This white swallow-tailed flag is divided vertically by three wavy lines. In heraldic terms, a wavy line, or udly, represents water. The lines may either represent the Clyde, one of Britain's most important rivers for trade and shipbuilding or, equally, the three partners who formed the company in 1956. The red serif 'H' is cleverly superimposed on the lines in imitation of a bridge across a river.

    Harrisons (Clyde) Ltd was a ship management company. Its predecessor company, Gow, Harrison and Co., was formed from an amalgamation of Allan C. Gow and Co. and P.H. Dixon and Co. This modern design is in complete contrast to the more traditional house flag of Gow, Harrison and Co., Glasgow. Illustrated in [Lloyd's Book of House Flags and Funnels](#) (1912), the design is a blue saltire dividing a white rectangular field. The initials 'G H & Co' in red serif appear in each check, the white disc in the centre features a heraldic red lion.

FLAG WAVES

Most flags, including house flags, are rectangular in shape and their design follows a traditional heraldic format. The basic division of a field is created by horizontal or vertical lines. Here the field is divided in quarters, or quadrisections, which in vexolological terms are described as 'checks'. There is no evidence explaining why the Hindustan Steam Shipping Co. flag is quartered in blue, yellow, white and red.

    It was not uncommon for shipping companies to change their names. The Hindustan Steam Shipping Co. was originally registered as J.W. Squance and Co. in Sunderland in 1893 by Captain Squance and Francis Common. Following the retirement of Captain Squance in 1906, the company changed its name to Common Brothers Ltd. The rectangular flag quartered in blue, yellow, white and red was used by both Common Brothers and the Hindustan Steam Shipping Co. — named after the first ship they purchased.

Hindustan Steam Shipping Co. Ltd
House flag, Newcastle-upon-Tyne, c. 1951
unknown maker, machine sewn
111.7 × 182.9 cm

FLAG WAVES

H. Hogarth & Sons
House flag, Glasgow, c. 1951
unknown maker, machine sewn
121.9 × 182.9 cm

Alfred Holt & Co. Ltd (formed 1865, trading as Blue Funnel Line)
House flag, Liverpool, *c.* 1951,
unknown maker, machine sewn
83.8 × 137.1 cm

FLAG WAVES

Houlder Brothers and Co. (formed 1856)
House flag, London, c. 1951
unknown maker, machine sewn
116.8 × 182.9 cm

The highly original design of the Silvertown flag employs the basic tenets of flag design. However, in place of a line, a white telegraph cable divides the rectangular red field diagonally. A white dove in flight carrying an olive branch in its beak is in the upper right half of the field, while two clasped hands occupy the lower left. In using the universal symbols of peace and friendship, the flag transcends both geographical and language boundaries like the company's submarine telegraph cables.

Silvertown Telegraph Company was a subsidiary of the India Rubber Gutta Percha and Telegraph Works Company. Founded by Samuel Silver in 1854, it was one of the first factories to be established in Silvertown, an area on the north bank of the Thames opposite Woolwich. S.W. Silver manufactured waterproof clothing in Greenwich before moving to Silvertown, giving his name to the new suburb. The company diversified into cable manufacture. In 1865, it laid its first cable, which ran from Dover to Cap Gris Nez. Two years later a cable was laid under the Gulf of Mexico, linking Havana via Key West Punta Rassa in Florida. In 1887 The Telegraphist reported that 'The area of ground covered by these important works at Silvertown is about fifteen acres, the floor-area of the workshops being about ten acres, and the total number of engineers and work-people engaged in telegraph work and the manufacture of India-rubber goods is rarely less than 2,800'.

India Rubber Gutta Percha and Telegraph Works Co. Ltd (Silvertown Telegraph Co.)
House flag, London, *c.* 1911
unknown maker, painted, machine sewn
124.5 × 177.8 cm

Iraq Petroleum Co. (formed 1929)
House flag, London, c. 1955–1967
unknown maker, painted, machine sewn
38.1 × 66 cm

The pale blue pennant of the Iraq Petroleum Co. is a simple but effective design. A disc with wavy black and gold stripes forms the lower half, the upper half is white. A narrow gold isosceles triangle rising from the stripes represents drilling activities. The logo of the company is painted onto the pennant. A similar but less stylised design of an oil rig emerging from water with two sails and a sun has been used for the flag of the Basra Governorate.

The Iraq Petroleum Co. was incorporated in 1912 as the Turkish Petroleum Company and the partnership included the British Anglo-Persian Oil Company, Royal Dutch Shell and Calouste Gulbenkian. It secured a petroleum concession agreement to explore and produce oil in the then Ottoman province of Mesopotamia around Mosul and Baghdad. In 1929 it became the Iraq Petroleum Company and entered into a formal partnership with the Near East Development Corporation, an American consortium of five large US oil companies. During the 1960s, the Iraq government increasingly objected to the Western ownership of the company, and it was nationalised in 1972.

FLAG WAVES

Commissioners of Irish Lights
Flag, before 1970
unknown maker, painted, machine sewn
124.4 × 182.8 cm

The Commissioners of Irish Lights is the lighthouse authority for all the island of Ireland, its adjacent seas and islands. It is a cross-border organisation with its headquarters in Dublin. A new version of this flag, introduced in September 1970, has the cross of St Patrick instead of that of St George.

94

FLAG WAVES

Isle of Man Steam Packet Co. Ltd (formed 1829)
House flag, Douglas, Isle of Man, c. 1951
unknown maker, machine sewn
88.9 × 134.6 cm

King Line Ltd
House flag, London, c. 1951
unknown maker, printed, machine sewn
121.9 × 182.9 cm

The emblem is derived from the coat of arms of the Philipps family, owners of the company and irreverently called by staff 'a puppy dancing on a sausage'.

FLAG WAVES

Throughout the 19th and 20th centuries geometric forms were used by numerous mercantile companies in a variety of ways. Lambert Brothers white rectangular flag with a red equilateral triangle in the centre is listed in Lloyd's Book of House Flags and Funnels (1912). A white inverted triangle on a red field was employed within a military context to denote a veterinary hospital.

Historically coal was transported by sea. In the 19th century, nearly all London homes were heated by coal. The two Lambert brothers were members of The Coal Factors' Society (established 1761), which protected the interests of individuals engaged in the wholesale coal trade. They were based in the Coal Exchange, an imposing Victorian building on Thames Street in the City of London, close to Billingsgate. As well as being a fish market, Billingsgate also traded coal. By 1896, the Lambert Brothers operated a fleet of ten coastal colliers. However, the same year they sold their fleet to William Corry and turned their interests to tramp steamers. In 1923 Lambert Brothers became substantial shareholders of the Temple Steam Ship Company.

Lambert Brothers Ltd
House flag, London, *c.* 1951
unknown maker, machine sewn
121.9 × 182.9 cm

FLAG WAVES

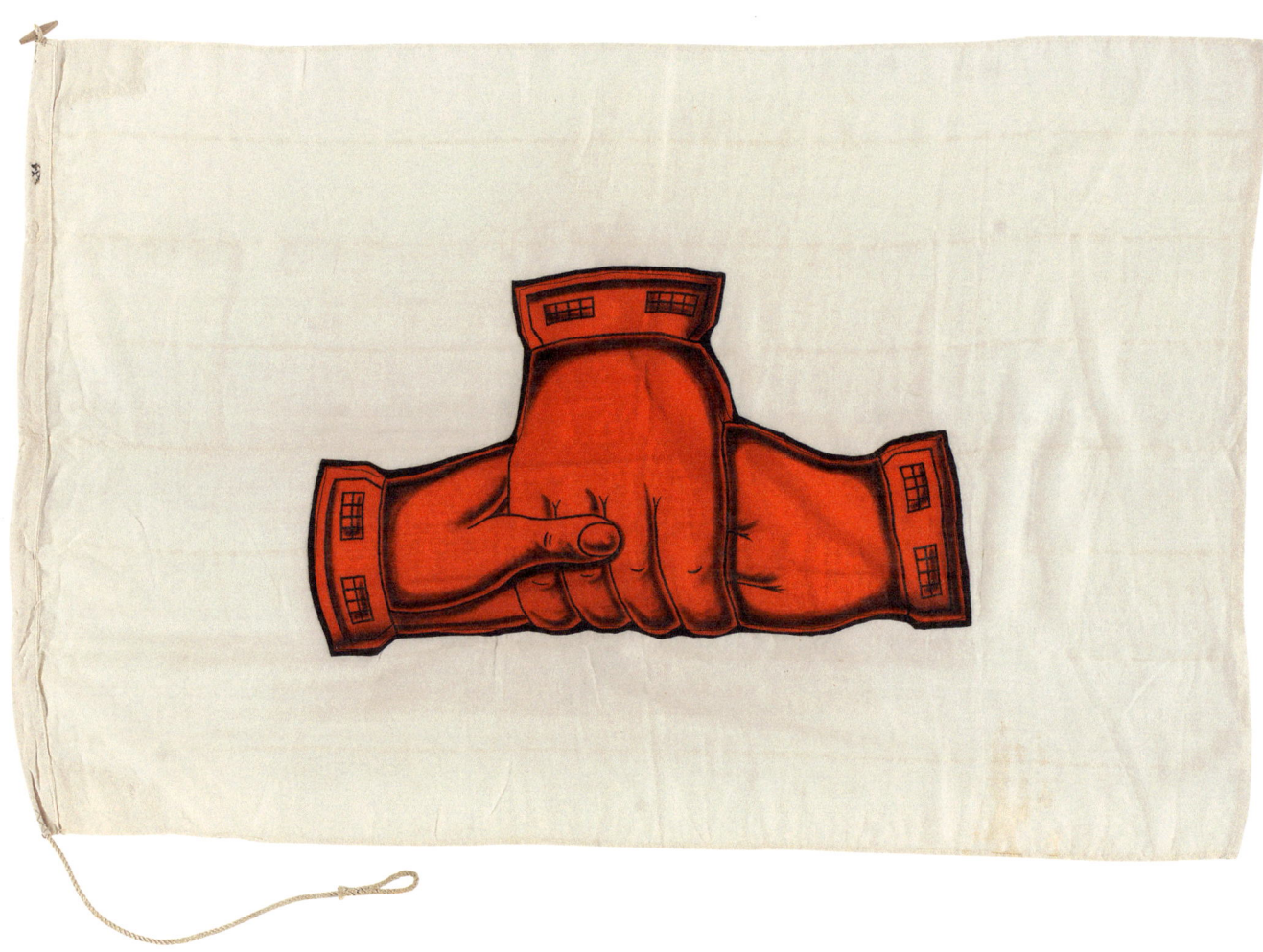

Larrinaga Steamship Co.
House flag, Liverpool, *c.* 1955
unknown maker, printed, machine sewn
116.8 × 185.4 cm

The flag is said to represent a hand shake between the three partners confirming the decision to run steam services through the Suez Canal or alternatively the three Basque families who founded the firm Olano, Larrinaga and De Longa. The design was in use from the 1860s until 1974.

Link Line Ltd
House flag, Liverpool, c. 1955–1967
unknown maker, machine sewn
124.4 × 182.9 cm

The rectangular white flag bearing a black tower and crescent is based on the original house flag in Lloyd's Book of House Flags and Funnels (1912). Castles and crescents were popular motifs in heraldry. This is a more modern version of the original, which gives the impression of a woodcut.

    The Court Line tramp shipping company was founded in 1905 by Philip Edward Haldenstein and based in London. During the First World War, and in response to anti-German feeling, Haldenstein changed his name to Halden. Court Line ships were all named after country houses with the suffix 'Court', for example Arlington Court. The fleet greatly expanded in the 1920s, and by 1926 it comprised 26 ships. Lawrence Philipps joined the company in 1929 to form Halden and Philipps. However, the company was badly affected by the Great Depression and during the Second World War it lost 13 ships to enemy action. The company moved into bulk carriers and tankers in the 1960s, changing its prefix from 'Court' to 'Halcyon'. The company's diversification into airlines, shipbuilding and repairs was unsuccessful and it went into liquidation in 1974.

London Court Line Ltd
House flag, c. 1955–1967
unknown maker, machine sewn
121.9 × 167.6 cm

FLAG WAVES

Manchester Ship Canal Co. Ltd
House flag, Manchester, c. 1955–1967
unknown maker, machine sewn
101.6 × 187.9 cm

FLAG WAVES

Thames barge MEMORY
Name pennant, 1904
unknown maker, machine sewn
185.4 × 594.3 cm

FLAG WAVES

The imposing Port of Liverpool Building, together the Royal Liver Building and Cunard Building (Liverpool's Three Graces) dominate the city's waterfront. The Mersey Docks and Harbour Board (MDHB) flag does not, however, take inspiration from the maritime themes which decorate the building. The white rectangular flag is divided diagonally by a thick wavy line which represents the River Mersey. In the upper right a red liver bird holding a branch of laver seaweed gazes across the river towards a six-pointed black star with wavy rays. The mythological liver pool is the iconic symbol of Liverpool, two of the cormorant-like birds, Bella and Bertie, grace the clock towers of the Royal Liver Building. A six-pointed star appears on the Coat of Arms of Birkenhead.

The MDHB was formed in 1858 to oversee the running of Liverpool's docks. It also managed the dock's network of railways which totalled some 104 miles of lines. These facilitated traffic from the passenger liners to Liverpool's intercity rail terminals. Until 1994 MDHB's offices were based at the Port of Liverpool Building at the Pier Head.

Mersey Docks & Harbour Board
House flag, Liverpool, unknown date
unknown maker, machine sewn
121.9 × 185.4 cm

FLAG WAVES

Metcalf Motor Coasters Ltd (originally part of C. Crawley Ltd, formed 1893)
House flag, London, *c.* 1951
unknown maker, machine sewn
132 × 182.8 cm

108

FLAG WAVES

National Maritime Museum
Flag, c. 1957
unknown maker, machine sewn
167.6 × 269.2 cm

This design was in use from 1957 until May 1974.

109

FLAG WAVES

Niarchos Ltd (formed 1952)
House flag, London, c. 1955
unknown maker, machine sewn
121.9 × 182.8 cm

North Thames Gas Board
House flag, London, c. 1951
unknown maker, machine sewn
167.6 × 228.6 cm

FLAG WAVES

North Yorkshire Shipping Co. Ltd (formed 1954)
House flag, *c.* 1955–1967
unknown maker, printed, machine sewn
152.4 × 215.9 cm

112

Orkney Steam Navigation Co. (formed 1868)
House flag, Kirkwall, c.1955–1967
unknown maker, machine sewn
86.3 × 132 cm

FLAG WAVES

Osborn and Wallis (formed 1880)
House flag, Cardiff, c. 1951
unknown maker, machine sewn
124.4 × 185.4 cm

Overseas Containers Ltd
House flag, London, *c.* 1955–1967
unknown maker, machine sewn
114.3 × 182.8 cm

This red wool burgee is printed with a black skull and crossbones. The 'Jolly Roger' had been used since the 18th century to signal when pirates were about to attack. It was flown by Lieutenant William Colbeck, who was a member of the Pirate Yacht Club. Colbeck was part of the crew of the SS <u>Southern Cross</u>, which left Hobart in Tasmania for Antarctica in 1898. He flew the flag on the sledge journey across the pack ice of the Ross Sea, taking 43 days.

The flag has since been mounted on card, framed and inscribed: 'Burgee flown by Lieutenant Wm. Colbeck R.N.R., F.R.G.S, a member of the Pirate Yacht Club on Sledge journey across the Great Ice Barrier when in company with C.E. Borchgrevink F.R.G.S, the farthest South was attained Lat. 78° 50′ S. Long. 164° 30′ W. on 17 February 1900. The sledge was detached from S.Y. "Southern Cross" Southern Cross expedition of which Lieutenant Colbeck was Chief Magnetic Observer'. A further note on the mount states 'Previous farthest south 78° 10′ by Capt Ross'.

The Royal Yorkshire Yacht Club (RYYC) was established in 1847. Queen Victoria was a patron and the club was allowed to wear the red ensign and burgee defaced with the Queen's crown and white rose of York. The Pirate Yacht Club, Bridlington resigned from the RYYC in 1898 and pursued a more egalitarian approach to yacht racing. The RYYC subsequently revised the rules to allow open class yacht competitions and the Pirate Yacht Club voluntarily disbanded in 1906.

Pirate Yacht Club
Burgee, Bridlington, c. 1898
unknown maker, printed, machine sewn
38.1 × 63.5 cm

FLAG WAVES

Blue flag with the badge of the Prince of Wales
Flag early 20th century,
unkown maker, printed, machine sewn
45.7 × 88.9 cm

118

FLAG WAVES

Silver Jubilee of Queen Elizabeth II
Flag, London Celebrations Committee, 1977
made by Benjamin Edgington Ltd, machine sewn
185.4 × 365.7 cm

FLAG WAVES

Queen Steam Fishing Co. Ltd (formed c. 1900)
House flag, Grimsby, c.1955–1967
unknown maker, machine sewn
137.1 × 172.7 cm

Regent Petroleum Tankship Co. Ltd (formed 1947)
House flag, London, c. 1955
made by Benjamin Edgington Ltd, printed, machine sewn
134.6 × 213.3 cm

Royal Mail
Pennant, after 1952
unknown maker, printed, machine sewn
162.5 × 330.2 cm

Sheaf Steam Shipping Co. Ltd (founded 1906)
House flag, Newcastle upon Tyne, c. 1951
unknown maker, printed, machine sewn
91.4 × 134.6 cm

FLAG WAVES

Shell Tankers Ltd
House flag, c. 1955–1967
unknown maker, machine sewn
147.3 × 322.5 cm

This red rectangular flag with a white disc in the centre bearing a gold shell adheres to a conventional house flag design, replacing the letter of the company with the iconic Shell logo. The Shell Transport and Trading Company initially used a mussel shell as its logo in 1901 but this was changed to the familiar scallop shell in 1904. The bright red and yellow colours were allegedly chosen by the Shell Company of California in 1915 to indicate the state's close ties with Spain (red and yellow are the colours of the Spanish flag). In 1971, the industrial designer Raymond Loewy produced a simplified version of the logo. He also designed logos for BP and Exxon.

    The Shell Group began as a small trading company founded by London businessman Marcus Samuel. His business originally traded small gifts and antiques, specialising in boxes decorated with seashells purchased from merchant seamen travelling back from the Far East. The business expanded to include general merchandise and, by 1892, was exporting Russian kerosene to Far East ports, carried by one of the world's first oil tankers, the [Murex](). The murex is a predatory tropical marine mollusc and Samuel would subsequently name all of his kerosene tankers after seashells.

FLAG WAVES

Ship Towage Ltd (formed 1950)
House flag, London, c. 1955–1967
unknown maker, machine sewn
116.8 × 182.8 cm

South Eastern Gas Board
House flag, unknown date
unknown maker, machine sewn
68.6 × 116.8 cm

FLAG WAVES

Stag Line Ltd
House flag, North Shields, c. 1955–1967
unknown maker, painted, machine sewn
147.3 × 213.3 cm

The design dates from 1846 when the company purchased its first vessel, a wooden snow named Stag.

Stanhope Steamship Co. Ltd (formed 1934)
House flag, London, *c.* 1955–1967
unknown maker, machine sewn
114.3 × 185.4 cm

FLAG WAVES

Stevinson, Hardy & Co. Ltd
House flag, London, c. 1955–1967
unknown maker, machine sewn
116.8 × 187.9 cm

FLAG WAVES

Strick Line Ltd
House flag, London, c. 1955
unknown maker, machine sewn
149.8 × 203.2 cm

Southampton, Isle of Wight and South of England Royal Mail Steam Packet Company Ltd
House flag, c. 1955–1967
unknown maker, machine sewn
81.3 × 124.4 cm

Formed by merger in 1861, the company now operates as Red Funnel ferries.

Stirling Shipping is the offshore division of Harrisons (Clyde) Ltd and the house flag is very similar. The rectangular flag is divided vertically twice, the outer stripes are red and the middle stripe is white. The middle stripe is divided by two narrow, wavy vertical blue lines running parallel. The distillation of elements of the Harrisons flag into this bold design also plays on the concept of the red, white and blue of the British ensign. A concept entirely fitting for an offshore company.

Stirling Shipping Company Ltd was a private offshore company that serviced oil and gas platforms in the North Sea. It operated a fleet of nine platform supply vessels, which serviced drilling and production facilities and supported offshore construction work. Stirling Shipping also operated three vessels used for towing rigs and manoeuvring anchors into position.

Stirling Shipping Co. Ltd
House flag, Glasgow, 1986
unknown maker, machine sewn
185.4 × 119.4 cm

FLAG WAVES

Board of Trade Blue Ensign
Flag, unknown date
unknown maker, printed, machine sewn
180.3 × 370.8 cm

Corporation of Trinity House
Flag, c. 1910
unknown maker, painted, machine sewn
116.8 × 154.9 cm

Trinity House is the General Lighthouse Authority for England, Wales, the Channel Islands and Gibraltar and a charity dedicated to safeguarding shipping and seafarers.

The original house flag of the Tyne Tees Steam Shipping Company (TTSSC) was a rectangle divided into four parts by a white saltire. The top and bottom triangles were red, the hoist and fly triangles were blue. The initials of the company 'TT', 'S' 'Co.' and 'S' were placed in the centre of each triangle (reading clockwise from top). This red rectangular flag with a yellow crest of a rampant lion on a tower holding a banner is described as the house flag of TTSSC. Within the language of heraldry, the lion symbolises courage, royalty or nobility, loyalty and valour. The motif of a lion atop a castle holding a banner of the red cross of St George appears on the coat of arms of Newcastle. However, the flag appears to be an anomaly. It does not appear to derive from the original illustrated in Lloyd's Book of House Flags and Funnels (1912), nor does it appear to be a derivation of the Coast Lines house flag, a rectangular flag with five horizontal stripes comprising blue at the top and bottom, and a central red stripe between two white stripes. The blue letters 'CL' are placed across the centre. The flag forms part of the Pope Collection and may have been misidentified.

The Tyne Tees Steam Shipping Company operated passenger services from Newcastle-upon-Tyne and Sunderland to London and the Continent from 1904 to 1943. It was formed from an amalgamation of four companies: the Tyne Steam Shipping Co. Ltd, the Tees Union Steamship Co. Ltd, the Free Trade Wharf Co. Ltd, and Furness Withy and Co. Ltd. In 1943 Tyne Tees Steam Shipping Company was purchased by Coast Lines, which provided shipping services across the United Kingdom, Ireland and the Channel Islands.

Tyne Tees Steam Shipping Co. Ltd
House flag, Newcastle-upon-Tyne, c. 1955–1967
unknown maker, machine sewn
137.1 × 215.9 cm

FLAG WAVES

Ulster Steamship Co. Ltd
House flag, Belfast, c. 1951
unknown maker, machine sewn
88.9 × 142.2 cm

The Ulster Steamship Company house flag appears in the 1912 edition of <u>Lloyd's Book of House Flags and Funnels</u>. The company retained the original design of a blue rectangular flag bearing a white shield with the red hand of Ulster dripping blood. The white initials 'U.S.S. Co' are placed near the hoist. The 'red hand of Ulster' is a traditional heraldic device which has been in use at least since the 13th century. It is usually shown as a right hand, however on the flag it is depicted as a left hand. Several legends exist as to the original of the 'red hand'. It is likely that the symbol was originally used on a banner depicting victory in battle, signalling divine intervention and strength.

    The Ulster Steamship Company was registered in 1877. The company ran services to the east coast of Canada, the Far East, Europe and Baltic Ports. Voyages to New Orleans began in 1896 when the company began carrying a limited number of passengers. In 1917 it took over the Irish Shipowners Company Ltd (Thomas Dixon & Sons, Belfast), known as Lord Line, which ran sailings between Belfast, Dublin, Cardiff and Baltimore as well as Rotterdam to Galveston and Cardiff to Montreal and Quebec.

The white rectangular flag with a fouled anchor placed aslant is based on that of the East Asiatic Company of which the United Baltic Corporation (UBC) was originally a subsidiary. The flag retains the white field of the original but changed the colour of the anchor from blue to red. The letters of the parent company have been replaced by san serif 'UBC'. In nautical terms, 'foul' means to entangle or that something is amiss. It was the personal seal of Lord Howard of Effingham, Lord High Admiral under Elizabeth I and James I, and has been adopted as a naval emblem ever since. In practical terms, a fouled anchor is something to be avoided and its heraldic use is purely a matter of aesthetics.

   The United Baltic Corporation (UBC) was founded in 1919 as a partnership between the East Asiatic Company, Copenhagen and Andrew Weir and Co., London. It was established to run passenger and cargo ships between the Baltic and London. Emigrants from Eastern Europe would often use the UBC's ships as the first leg in their journey to America. The Second World War disrupted the service. Post-war, the company resumed operations in Poland as well as a new service to Finland. However, it sold its last passenger ship in 1947 to concentrate on cargo services.

United Baltic Corporation Ltd
House flag, c. 1951
unknown maker, machine sewn
114.3 × 190.5 cm

FLAG WAVES

United Towing Ltd (formed 1920)
House flag, Hull, c. 1955–1967
unknown maker, machine sewn
119.4 × 210.8 cm

144

United Towing Salvage
House flag, c. 1955–1967
unknown maker, printed, machine sewn
86.3 × 142.2 cm

FLAG WAVES

Western Ferries (Clyde) Ltd
House flag, Glasgow, 1985
unknown maker, machine sewn
185.4 × 119.4 cm

The rectangular blue flag with white disc in the centre bears the Western Ferries red logo pointing in opposite directions attached to a circle. Its antecedents can be seen in the simple designs of many house flags from the 19th and early 20th centuries.

Western Ferries operates a vehicle and passenger service between the islands on the west coast of Scotland. The company was founded in 1968 by a small group of Scottish businessmen and initially operated between Kennacraig, West Loch Tarbert and Islay. As business and tourism increased, the company expanded, adding more ships to the fleet and increasing sailings. In 1985 the company was restructured becoming Western Ferries (Clyde) Ltd. Each ship is named after a sound (large sea or ocean inlet) of Scotland.

Wyre Trawlers
House flag, Fleetwood, c. 1955–1967
unknown maker, machine sewn
142.2 × 210.8 cm

FLAG WAVES

Skull and crossbones
Flag, c. 1957
unknown maker, machine sewn
200 × 167 cm

Made for the film Windjammer.

150

Zillah Shipping Co. Ltd (formed 1949)
House flag, Liverpool, unknown date
unknown maker, machine sewn
119.4 × 172.7 cm

Published in 2021 by Four Corners Books
56 Artillery Lane, London E1 7LS

NATIONAL MARITIME MUSEUM GREENWICH

The National Maritime Museum is the world's largest maritime museum, telling stories of Britain's epic relationship with the sea — global encounters, cultural exchange and human endurance.

All text and images © National Maritime Museum
rmg.co.uk

This volume © Four Corners Books 2021

Distributed in the UK and Europe by Art Data
artdata.co.uk

page 10, excerpts from the poem Flag by John Agard, from Half-Caste and Other Poems, reproduced by permission of Hodder Children's Books, an imprint of Hachette Children's Books, Carmelite House, 50 Victoria Embankment, London, EC4Y 0DZ

Designed by Claire Mason
flushleft.co.uk

Print Production by Martin Lee

Image Reproduction by Flavio Milani

Printed in Italy by Printer Trento

ISBN: 978-1-909829-17-6

fourcornersbooks.co.uk

ACKNOWLEDGEMENTS

The publisher would like to thank all those at the National Maritime Museum, Greenwich who worked on this project and helped to make it possible: Sue Prichard, Rochelle Bisson, Sarah Connelly, Kirsty Schaper and everyone involved in photographing the flags, including the teams from the photographic studio, conservation and collection management. The author would like to thank Dr Robert Blyth.